CASSIUS KING

Edited by Kristen Corrects, Inc.

Cover art design by Ebenezer O. Makinde

Character sketch design by Alex Woolery

First edition published 2023

CASSIUS KING

EBENEZER O. MAKINDE

CHAPTER 1

Cassius walked carefully to the line of scrimmage, his offensive linemen already crouching in their three-point stances, ready to shoot across the line and take on the defense at the snap of the football. The wind was now blowing hard, and by the looks of the grayish, puffy clouds, rain was not far off, either.

It was the fourth quarter, with just forty seconds to play, and the Warhawks, the undefeated Little League pee-wee football team that Cassius quarterbacked, was facing a situation they hadn't encountered all season—down by six points deep into the fourth quarter. As a matter of fact, they hadn't been down all year, but today the Trojans, the team lined up across from them, were in dire need of a win to close out the regular season, in hopes of gaining some momentum for the next one. For them, the playoffs were completely out of the question, and so a consolation win over the premier team in the Mighty Might football conference would be the apex of a season that until now had been nothing beyond subpar.

Even though the Trojans, with their red and black uniforms, were much smaller and less experienced than Cassius and the black-and-gold Warhawks, they had prepared harder that week than they had for any other game before, even meeting the previous night to watch film at the head coach's house, a rare occasion. It seemed to have paid off, as until that point they had limited the Warhawks to a measly six points, and had not allowed them to surpass one hundred yards rushing, a rare feat considering Cassius and the fleet-footed Warhawks had averaged more than three hundred yards on the ground the entire season. But somehow, they had rallied hard and played their hearts out, and were on pace to land one of the biggest upsets of the year.

For the Warhawks, the stakes were high and this game meant everything. If they won, they would secure their first-ever bid to the regional championship games that would bring in all of the top teams throughout the northwest for a weekend showdown of tournament football to decide on a champion. It was something they had dreamed about all season, a chance to be able to showcase their skills at the highest level and in front of the biggest audience. And indeed, the scale was large—the games this year would be held in succession, one after another on the Blue, Boise State's famous blue turf. For Cassius, it was more than a dream come true: Since he was a child, he'd dreamed of not only playing on the blue turf as a pee-wee football player, but of also donning the blue and orange and playing for his favorite squad as a collegiate athlete. His bedroom did nothing to hide this fact; jerseys of some of his favorite players—Kellen Moore, Doug Martin, Jamar Taylor—covered every inch of his wall. When he said his prayers just before going to sleep at night, he squeezed his Fiesta Bowl autographed Boise State football, just as he solidified his prayers with a joyful amen. He knew that playing on that field was his destiny, and since the day he attended his first game a few years back, he was determined to do whatever it took to make his dream a reality.

Now, he had his chance. A win, and his Warhawks squad would be given a chance to compete on the Blue—fulfilling the first part of his dream. All they had to do now was what seemed to be impossible: score a touchdown with forty seconds left to play, all the way from their own thirty-five-yard line. The small crowd of parents and children, usually loud and vibrant cheering on their Warhawks, now stood quietly on the sideline as the entire season hung in the balance.

*

Cassius—despite the wind, the pressure, the silence from the crowd—calmly approached the line of scrimmage as he had done so many times before, scanning the defense's position, ready to adjust the play call where needed. As he placed his hands under Bones, his gritty center and his best friend, he lifted his leg to send Kareem, his gangly, playmaking receiver, into motion.

"Set HUT! Set HUT!" he shouted, trying to get the aggressive defense to jump off sides, and also to get them to show their true coverage. Just as he had suspected, the defense had been bluffing cover two, only willing to reveal it at the snap of the football. Now knowing the Trojans were playing only one man high, man coverage, he took a step back and shifted his eyes to the sideline, where the offensive coordinator and head coach, Coach King, stood with his hands raised, ready to change the play call. The clock was ticking down for them to get the play off—and they couldn't afford to take a penalty that would move them back another five yards.

Ten. Nine. Eight. Seven...

Coach King quickly signaled in a new play, and Cassius stepped back and relayed the call to the rest of his teammates. The tight end to his right repositioned as a wideout to his left, and Kareem took a step forward, now putting himself on the line of scrimmage. Three receivers stood to Cassius's left, with only Kareem to his right—just what Coach King, the Warhawks, and especially Cassius and the Human Highlight Reel, Kareem, wanted.

Three. Two. One...

At the last second, Cassius put his hand under center and tapped Bones to snap the football. He dropped back in the pocket, knowing that the Trojan pass rush had been on him all game, and he would need to move quickly to avoid a sack, look off the safety, allowing Kareem to get true single coverage downfield, and for him to let fly a decent ball to allow for his star to make a play.

As he dropped back, it was as if everything around him stood still—he couldn't hear a sound or see any other distraction around him. It was just him and the football.

As he took that fifth step, he saw that the defensive line had crossed two of their linemen, which had succeeded in getting one of them free, and now number ninety-nine, the Trojans' best defender, was coming directly at him. He had no time to look off the safety now—he had to just let the ball fly.

He took a few steps to his right, located Bones screaming downfield, and let fly what Coach King called the "Big Dipper," a high arching ball that allowed for a great receiver to make a play.

Just as he let it fly, number ninety-nine got to him, delivering a solid hit that sent Cassius tumbling to the ground. Instinctively, he turned over to face downfield, to see if Bones could make the big play. Bones, with his above-average speed, separated himself and the cornerback, but still had the safety closing in on him at an angle. But the angle was bad, and Cassius could see that as long as he hadn't overthrown him, the ball would not be intercepted.

He held his breath for what seemed like an eternity as Bones pumped his arms to race down the ball. Could he do it?

As the ball began its descent, it appeared that Cassius had overthrown him, and that the ball would drop down, incomplete, bringing about a long fourth down. But, Bones was Bones, and with all of his playmaking ability, he stretched at the last second, tipped the ball with his fingers, and pulled it in. A miraculous catch. Because he was so off balance, although the safety trailed him by a few steps, he stumbled his way down to the one-yard line, just short of a touchdown.

Cassius got to his feet and immediately signaled to the referee for a timeout, stopping the clock at just eighteen seconds. It was the Warhawks' final timeout. They were down six, and they needed a score and a field goal to win.

The team ran to the sideline with joy, slapping Bones on the shoulder pads for making an incredible catch. The players, ecstatic, were now close to doing the impossible—the world-famous Blue Turf at the forefront of their minds.

"Hey! Hey!" Coach King scolded the boys as they reached the sideline. "We're not done yet, are we? Still gotta punch this in. Focus up, gentlemen!" He sent each of the players a fierce gaze.

Realizing their coach was right, the players ceased and refocused their attention.

"All right, let's play ball," Coach King said. "Eighteen seconds left, down by six, the game is on the line. You already know what's at stake. Right now is our time, Warhawks, right now. We need just one yard, and that's it. Don't focus on the Blue, don't focus on your friends or your family—focus on the here and now, and we'll get the job done."

Coach King went silent, scanning over his players, looking each in the eye. The huddle was so silent you could have probably heard a pin drop.

"Nothing fancy, fellas," he began again, now fixing his eyes on Cassius. "Quarterback sneak. You want it, you go get it. Unbalanced right, 24 QB blast."

The Warhawks players nodded, accepting that it was now or never, and acknowledging that Coach King had called a quarterback sneak. The pressure was on the offensive line with Bones as the center, and Cassius to come up with the game-tying play.

The referee blew the whistle, signaling that the timeout

was over, and the teams should retake the field.

As the Warhawks jogged back to the one-yard line to take their positions, Rimar, the bowling ball running back who would be lining up behind Cassius, gave him a slap on the shoulder and whispered in his ear, "Get us in, Captain. But if you don't, I'll be there to push you in."

The Warhawks got to the huddle, and all eyes were fixed on Cassius as he took a few deep breaths before calling the play. He thought of all his hopes and dreams and how this play could be the beginning of realizing them. He thought about the posters of his favorite players on his wall. At one time or another, they had each walked in his shoes as pee-wee football players.

He closed his eyes and said a quick prayer, as he had done before other big moments, and just as he'd done every night before he squeezed his lucky Boise State football before bed.

Looking up at his teammates once again, he smiled and whispered, "Boise…"

They smiled back and responded in a quiet voice, "State…"

"All right boys, let's punch this in. Unbalanced right, 24 QB blast. On BALL. Ready…"

"Break!" the entire huddle responded, clapping as one heartbeat.

The lineman sprinted to the line, as they had always done, dropping their hands and getting into their stances. Cassius walked to the line, again surveying the defensive, seeing that they had all scrunched together over Bones. There was no mistake what was coming. Whoever's will was stronger in the next play would be the winner. The Warhawks had no timeouts, so if they didn't get in, they'd have to spike the ball to give them another chance.

But to Cassius, that wasn't an option—nothing would stop him from getting in, from playing on the Blue turf.

He straddled his legs, giving himself a wide base to plunge forward. He tapped Bones, signaling the silent count and for him to snap the football. As soon as he felt it graze his fingers, he angled right, away from number ninety-nine, and toward a weaker defender. For a few seconds there was a struggle, and Cassius found himself stuck behind the line, driving his feet as hard as he could. The Trojans had done a great job of fortifying the line of scrimmage, and it seemed that the wall they'd created was hopelessly impenetrable.

Cassius closed his eyes and tried to will his way forward. But at that moment, something amazing happened—he felt a helmet and a set of shoulder pads collide into his back, pushing him and the line forward and across the goal line.

The Warhawks had scored! The players jumped up and down in a rush of excitement.

The referees ran across the goal line with both hands raised confirming the touchdown, and the crowd went wild. Now all the Warhawks would need to do was seal the game with the extra point, and they would win.

Coach King signaled one finger high into the air, and the extra point team came rushing onto the field. Cassius, being the placeholder, removed from his pants a glove that would allow him to secure the ball on the place tee. Turning to Bones, the team's reliable kicker, he gave him a word of encouragement.

"Get us to the blue," he said.

"No doubt," Bones responded.

The Warhawks lined up for the extra point, and because of the Little League rules, they faced no oncoming rush from the Trojans—they were free to kick uncontested. Cassius took to a knee, Bones took three steps back, lined his hands up and down to the center of the goal post and took a deep breath, dropping his shoulders. Seeing that Bones was ready, Cassius looked to the center and opened his hand, signaling that he was ready.

The ball was snapped and Cassius caught it cleanly, placing it carefully on the tee. As Bones had done so many times before, he took three choppy steps and drilled it right down the center. Money.

The game was over, the Warhawks had won.

CHAPTER 2

That entire afternoon prior to his family's usual family dinner, Cassius was so elated he hadn't removed any of his gear. After the team had celebrated on the field, and afterward with a smaller group at Peter Piper Pizza, he had invited Bones and Kareem back to his house to throw the football in his backyard, and to watch that evening's Boise State home football game. He didn't want to miss a moment of the action, he told his parents, and though they didn't totally agree, they let him continue in his euphoria. Coach King—or simply Dad as Cassius called him when the two weren't on the field—was still beaming, thinking about his son scoring the game-winning touchdown. Deep down, he didn't really mind the fact that Cassius hadn't changed, but he knew it was really Mrs. King who, although she loved football just as much as her boys, was much less lenient when it came to protecting her dirty floors, and expressed her displeasure that Cassius hadn't washed up since the game's completion.

"Cash!" she called out from the kitchen, Mr. King close by. "Dinner will be served in a half hour. And you're not tasting any of this food until your brown butt has hit the shower."

Cassius could smell his favorite dinner being cooked: baked macaroni and cheese and pulled pork sandwiches, and as he sat there in his room staring up at the posters on his ceiling, dreaming about the regional tournament in a month's time on the world-famous Blue, he was more elated than ever. But he knew that his mother was serious, and in that moment, after he heard his stomach growl for the third time, he knew he'd better get showered up in time for the family's dinner. Besides, he looked forward to dinner with his parents—they made the conversation fun and light. He rolled out of his Buster Bronco-shaped bed, grabbed his towel and a pair of fresh clothes, and hurried to the shower.

CHAPTER 3

Dinner that evening was more satisfying than Cassius expected. The pulled pork and baked macaroni and cheese tasted so good when they touched his lips, he ate slower than usual in order to savor every bite. Not only was the food great, but his mother had taken the time to decorate the table with all blue and orange colors—a rarity given it was her dining room table, the dining room table, the one she loved so much she wouldn't even let any of Cassius's friends use it. The sight of it was really something special. As the three of them ate, Cassius reflected on the day and the game.

"And can you believe it, Dad? I wasn't nervous at all. I walked up to the line cool as a cucumber. Just like Brett and Kellen did. And the guys—the guys, Dad. They were looking at me like I was the leader. Even Rimar called me Captain. Isn't that something, Dad?"

Mr. King forked through his food, smiling and nodding as his son went on and on about the game. "It was great son, it really was. Your mother and I are so proud of you and everything you accomplished this season. You worked hard all year and it showed when it got down to crunch time."

Cassius smiled. "Thanks, Dad. Now time to dominate the Blue. Those other teams have no shot when they face me."

Mr. and Mrs. King went silent, their eyes widening.

"Cash, don't forge—" his mother began, but before she could finish Mr. King interrupted.

"Absolutely, son. Those guys are in trouble when they face you. Aren't they, hun?"

Mrs. King put down her fork and narrowed her eyes. Her eyebrow was raised, which only happened when she was upset. Mr. King's eyebrows raised in return, as Cassius obliviously continued fishing through his food.

"I guess so. Cash, you're going to do great. Who wants dessert?" she asked, shifting the subject.

"Depends, what are we having?" Cassius asked.

Mrs. King rose from the table and headed to the kitchen. "Well, because tonight is a special occasion, we are having quite the treat. Homemade chocolate chip cookies and French vanilla ice cream."

Cassius clasped his hands together as his eyes widened, all but falling out of his chair. Each of them were delightful, but the combination of the two was almost too much for him to fathom. He squirmed around in his seat with excitement.

As Mrs. King made her way to the kitchen, Mr. King also got up as well, grabbing his phone and flipping through his contacts.

"You're not going to stay for dessert, Dad?" Cassius asked.

"No son, I'll have to take a rain check on dessert, maybe tomorrow."

Mrs. King, knowing that her husband was up to something, stopped in the doorway to the dining room and looked

Mr. King up and down. "You? Skip out on dessert? Who are you and what did you do with my husband? None of your bank clients could possibly need you at this time. Tell them to call you Monday."

Mr. King looked at her and with a straight face and shook his head. "No honey, not any clients. I need to make a call to the coaches about the banquet next weekend. Something urgent came up that I need to address. I'll tell you about it later."

Mrs. King looked at her husband as if he had just fallen from the sky. It was almost nine p.m. and he was wanting to place phone calls to the other coaches. But why? Not knowing what else to do, she simply nodded and headed off to the kitchen to grab the dessert.

Cassius, who had just finished cleaning the remainder of food from his plate, put his fork and knife down and with pulled pork barbecue still on the corner of his lips he echoed, "BOISEEEEE… STATEEEE." He couldn't hold still, his mouth watering for the chocolate chip cookies and slow-churned vanilla ice cream, and even more, for the big tournament on the world-famous Blue turf in just one month's time.

CHAPTER 4

It was the day of the banquet, and all of the pee-wee players and their families gathered at the fun-filled Oasis Amusement Park to enjoy all of the games, rides, food, and festivities before heading into the large banquet hall Mr. King had booked. There, they would do the more formal reception where the players would be recognized and given awards for their astounding work during the season. There would be awards for special teams player of the year, best offensive player, best defensive player, best teammate, and finally the most valuable player of the team—all of them voted on by the head coaches, except for that of the best teammate, which, by tradition, would be voted on by all of the players.

Even as Cassius and the others enjoyed all of the festivities around the park, they couldn't help but wonder who would be the winner of each award. There was speculation, of course—some thought Cassius was a shoe-in for MVP and the best offensive player, while others thought that the award would go to Kareem, as the dynamic playmaking wide receiver who made Cassius's job seem easier time and time again. Or perhaps the coaches would pull a fast one and recognize the offensive line, anchored by Bones at center, saying they were the ones deserving of some recognition, given the fact that the offense had been explosive all season and dominated in both the run and pass game.

But everyone's speculation was just that—speculation. They would have to simply wait and see. But in addition to the award, all the boys looked forward to hearing more about the tournament that was just three weeks away, and when they would be leaving, where they would be staying, and hopefully which team in the five-game tournament they would be scheduled to play first. Up until that time, none had heard anything about it—including Cassius, as his dad hadn't brought it up.

So he, like the rest of the players, moved about the park with great anticipation, trying to enjoy the fact that they had unlimited passes to all of the coasters and a stipend for food, all the while knowing that there was much to be done and said later in the evening that it was almost impossible not to have it in the back of their minds. Because of this, Cassius, Bones, Kareem, and Rimar, usually a gregarious and talkative bunch, kept quiet and to themselves, checking the time to assure they wouldn't be late for the banquet. Deep down, they each hoped that they would be the recipient of some type of award.

CHAPTER 5

Fifteen minutes before the big banquet was to begin, all of the players had made their way into the main hall and had taken their seats. Oval tables were set up evenly throughout the room, adorned with the black and gold Warhawk colors. On each spot before them was a sealed envelope that sat neatly placed next to a napkin. The boys, as they sat waiting for the coaches to arrive—which seemed odd as they were running the meeting—wondered why there wasn't any food or drink waiting for them on their arrival. No trophies and medals adorned the tables up front. There were no smells of food in the air, no music being played through any of the speakers.

"Bones," Cassius asked, "what is this? Where is everybody?"

Bones shrugged as he finished off a piece of chocolate cake that he had brought into the banquet hall. Despite his nickname, Bones was always eating. "You tell me. Coach King is your dad. Where's he at?"

Cassius's guess was as good as his. He had no idea where his father, let alone the coaches, were, and in reflecting upon the entire day, he realized that he hadn't seen any of them in the amusement park. Where had they gone?

He turned to the door and saw it empty, except for one

lone worker whose job it was to greet the guests coming inside. He looked over his other shoulder, and he saw seated in the back his mother next to Bones's mother, chatting as they waited patiently, as if nothing were off. Cassius slumped in his chair and looked at the envelope before him, which read on the front DO NOT OPEN. He looked once again at his watch—it was just ten minutes until the expected start time.

Cassius heard a commotion coming over his shoulder, followed by a successive number of loud pops. Turning his head, he noticed all of the coaches filing in, dressed in clown suits with red noses, firing off small hand popper fireworks as they made their way to the front of the banquet hall. Carnival music accompanied their entrance. As all the kids watched, they each couldn't help but laugh. *What in the world is going on?* Cassius thought.

CHAPTER 6

After the music stopped, Coach King removed his shiny red nose and his colorful wig and approached the podium. Clearing his throat, he motioned for those in the back of the banquet hall to have a seat.

"Warhawks… Parents, families, and players. It's good to see everyone and I hope you all had a good time out there—I know I did. I'm sure you're wondering why on earth we are dressed like this. If you look around, you'll notice that this year's banquet looks much different than other years—no food, no awards, no music—or real music for that matter—and nothing congratulating any of you on the regular season. I'm sure you noticed, didn't you?"

All the kids in the audience nodded, though they were immensely confused.

"Before we move into what we are actually doing here, I'd like for each of you to sit up in your chairs and prepare to write down three of the things you're most looking forward to regarding our regional tournament on the Blue. The coaches will come around and hand each of you a pen and paper. Once you receive it, fold your paper and place the pen down."

There was a bit of movement and chatter among the boys—they weren't sure exactly why they had been asked to complete the task. Each coach made their way around to the tables and handed the players a pen and paper. Cassius took a few moments of his own and wrote the following down.

- Scoring a touchdown on the blue
- Winning the championship
- Getting a cool picture and autographs from some Boise State players and seeing the new facilities

Satisfied with what he'd written, he folded up the sheet of paper and placed it on the table. Slowly, the rest of his teammates finished and placed the folded papers onto the table.

"Okay," Coach King began, "how many of you struggled to complete this task?"

Each of the boys looked around the room; not a single hand was raised.

"No one? Great. Looks like we're batting a thousand. Anyone care to share?"

A few hands went up across the room. Coach King decided to pick Maverick first, who was the backup free safety.

"Well, I've never been to a Boise State game, so I'm excited to get to stand on the turf," he said.

"Thanks for sharing, Maverick. How many of you boys said the same thing, or something similar to it? About it being the first time you'll ever get to be on the Blue?"

A number of hands shot up. Bits and pieces of chatter

could be heard throughout the room.

"Very nice. Who else would like to share?" Coach King asked.

Another hand went up toward the back. This time it was that of Justin Jones, a talented newcomer who played both linebacker and defensive end.

"I'm excited to spend time with my family, Coach."

"Your family? Explain," Coach King responded, eager to hear more.

"Yeah. My mom and dad are separated but they've agreed to get together and join me on the trip. So it's pretty exciting."

Coach King nodded and scanned over the room.

"All right team, here's what we're going to do. Pass your papers to the left to Coach Smith and give us a second to look them over, sound good? Go ahead and pass them to the left."

The boys moved hesitatingly, but nevertheless obeyed. Coach Smith, the defensive coordinator and Bones's dad, was waiting at the end room for all of the papers to arrive. Once he'd received them, he and the other coaches gathered to review them. The coaches huddled together was a sight to see, given they were each oddly dressed up as clowns. After they had reviewed all the papers, Coach King again turned to the boys and addressed them directly.

"Boys, thank you for doing this—great job. We've got some good and bad news for you. The good news is that your coaches and I, as you can see, just participated in the annual Oasis calendar shoot to raise money for all the other youth sports in our valley. The theme this year, as you've probably guessed, was A Carnival of a Time. Every sale of the calendar next year will bring a percentage back to our team. This is great so we won't have to pay out of pocket for many of our expenses, including the new jerseys we'll be getting for next season. So that's the good news. Now, go ahead and open up the envelopes before you."

The boys all reached in front of them and grabbed the envelopes, tearing them open. On each of the cards was a number.

"The bad news is that we don't have the funds yet to make the regional trip as a team. If we're going to be able to go, each of you has two weeks to come up with the number written on your card."

There were wide eyes and gasps throughout the entire room. The boys looked at each other in disbelief. The amount listed on the card for each player was the same—$100. Being kids, they'd never even held that large of an amount. Was Coach King being serious? Were they really in jeopardy of not being able to play if they couldn't come up with the money? Many of the kids looked to the back of the room for their parents, who were sitting there, stoically, quietly observing.

"Don't look back there for your parents. I've spoken to each of them, and they've all agreed that if this trip is something you really want to do, if you really want to experience the things on the list that you've all written down, then you'll have to raise the money on your own. Fair and square."

The kids were all wide eyed. None of them had jobs.

"And the money, I might add, will not be coming in the

form of an allowance. Therefore no money will be given to you by any of your parents. You must go out and find someone else to pay you to do a job."

Rimar, who was sitting near the front and to the right, stood to his feet. "Coach, what are we supposed to do?"

"You gotta figure it out. You really want to go and compete, don't you?"

"Yeah."

"Then sit down and come up with a plan on how you're going to do it. One hundred dollars total. Seven bucks a day. Or the cost of two video games or a new pair of shoes. That's it."

"So what about the awards?" Bones asked.

"Like I said, things are different this year. We don't have the funds right now for awards. Everything is going to go toward the trip. Any other questions?" Mr. King's responses seemed to be becoming more and more blunt.

The kids were so in shock that not a single hand rose. After just a few seconds Coach King clapped his hands and dismissed the boys to their parents.

"Two weeks!" he yelled, as he and the other coaches cleaned up the banquet hall. Slowly, as the boys realized the coaches were not joking, they rose from their seats and found their parents in the back.

Cassius, who was more in shock than the others considering his parents hadn't said a single thing, stood up and waited for his dad to finish. His mom approached from behind and put a hand on his shoulder.

"Hey Mom," he began. "Why would Dad make all the guys raise their own money?"

"Cash," his mother began. "It wouldn't be fair if your teammates had to raise the money and you didn't. You've got to participate just like them."

Coach King walked by, signaling to the two that it was time to go. "That's right, son. You've gotta pull your own weight as well. Your mom and I will be here to guide you, but you've gotta pull your weight."

As the two headed toward the car, Cassius stood there, frozen. He had no idea what he was going to do.

CHAPTER 7

The car eased down the road as Cassius peered through the windows at the passing houses and trees. He pondered how his parents, his dad, could do such a thing to essentially rob him of his lifelong dreams. How could they be so unfair? What was he supposed to do?

"Mommm," he wailed in the passenger seat. Cassius and his mother had taken a separate car from Mr. King, who had arrived later at the park due to the fact that he needed to attend to coaches' business and calendar shoot.

"Cashhh?" she replied, mimicking his sulking mood.

"I don't get it. Do we have money? Why do I have to raise it myself?"

Mrs. King paused, navigating the road. "Son, sometimes things in life aren't a matter of simply getting them done and checking them off—they're about the principle behind them and the lessons you learn in the process."

Cassius couldn't understand what lesson could be learned from a canceled trip, which was exactly what would happen if he or the others weren't able to raise the money.

"What should I do?" Cassius asked.

"Cassius King, you heard your father."

Cassius slumped deeper into the passenger's seat and

leaned his forehead against the window.

"Put that brain of yours to work and think, Cassius. Think," his mother said, unwilling to accommodate his downcast demeanor.

They reached a busy stop sign intersection a few minutes from their neighborhood and Cassius noticed on the side of the road two kids running a lemonade stand. Lemonade, Cassius thought.

His mind started turning.

"Lemonade. Lemonade. Lemonade. I know what I'll do, I'll start a lemonade stand!"

Mrs. King didn't say a word, but just smiled. Cassius clapped his hands together with joy, a big smile beaming across his face. He now knew exactly what he was going to do.

CHAPTER 8

That weekend, Cassius embarked on a grand scheme—starting his own business by opening up a lemonade stand on his street corner. After deciding to pursue the idea during the car ride home, he eagerly began gathering the necessary items from the cupboard in his kitchen. He would use tap water and the old lemonade mix that had been stored in the pantry. It was the cheap brand, but to Cassius it didn't matter—he knew the people in his neighborhood, like Mrs. Courtson down the block, and Mr. Hyde across the street, or even Chad who lived three doors down, would be out doing their lawns during the weekend, and they would come over to purchase some of what he was selling. There was also Mr. Jamison, who lived another five houses down, who worked at his father's company. But the man was rather quiet, and he never came out on Saturdays to do his lawn. Instead, he had always hired someone to do it for him, which made him even less accessible. So, Cassius decided, he likely wouldn't be a customer.

The last item he grabbed was a bag of basic sugar, which he always added to his own lemonade when his mother would make it, usually about two or three scoops that made it just the right sweetness.

With his ingredients ready and set aside on the dining

room table, he contemplated what he would need next. Obviously he would need some type of table to hold all of the equipment—the container of lemonade, the napkins, and some cups and spoons too, for mixing. He rummaged through the cabinets, tossing aside other items to get to the bag of old plastic utensils sitting half empty from former house parties, birthdays, and other get-togethers.

After grabbing the cups, he went to the garage, where piled up next to the garage door was a set of fold-up chairs, which had been sitting so long that they were now covered with cobwebs and spiders. Using an old shoe from the corner, he dusted off the webs and spiders, then grabbed a chair and set it by the door. Taking a deep breath, he looked at the time—it was now almost seven a.m., the time when his parents and his neighbors would begin heading outside to do their lawns.

With a deep feeling of satisfaction, he ran into the house, ran upstairs, and jumped into the shower to clean himself up to look presentable for his first day of his lemonade business.

CHAPTER 9

After Cassius had washed and gotten dressed, downstairs he grabbed the ingredients to set up on the street corner just north of his driveway, the place where the most foot traffic came on a usual Saturday morning. As he raced back and forth from the house to the corner, hauling all of the ingredients, Cassius's dad sat in his big recliner chair, reading the morning newspaper.

"Son," he asked as Cassius raced by for the fourth time. "What are you doing?"

Cassius came to a screeching halt. "I'm doing my part to raise my share of the money so we can make it to the tournament."

Mr. King nodded in approval. "Let me know if you need any help." He flipped his newspaper open and went back to reading. "I'm always here to help."

Cassius was determined to succeed in his lemonade venture, and a part of him wanted to prove that he could do it on his own. How hard could it be? He wanted to be an example to his teammates to encourage each of them to do the same, and so he knew any outside help would ultimately weaken his intentions and purpose. He would forge full steam ahead and see how things went.

He knew deep down things would work out. They always did. He'd set up shop on the sidewalk and the customers would start flooding in. Neighbors who had been working on their lawns would see him, and being thirsty and tired from the day's work, would drop by to spend a few dollars for a cup of refreshing lemonade. It would be a win-win for everybody—Cassius would raise the money to help his team go on the trip, and those in the neighborhood would get a cool and refreshing drink, all while supporting a good cause.

Just five minutes shy of seven, Cassius had finally completed the setup. He topped off all of his efforts by grabbing a sheet of loose leaf paper, writing LEMONADE on it, and taping it to the front edge of the table. He took his seat behind the counter, waiting for his thirsty customers to arrive.

CHAPTER 10

Ten minutes into the start of his business, Cassius received his first interested customer. An older couple walking the neighborhood approached the stand and greeted Cassius with a warm smile.

"Hello, what's your name?"

"Cassius, Cassius King," he responded.

"It's nice to meet you, Cassius," the elderly woman said. "I see you've got something you're selling?"

Cassius nodded his head in approval, eager for a sale. "Yes, yes I do. I'm selling lemonade, and it's for a good cause."

The older couple smiled politely, but just kept walking by.

"How nice," Cassius could hear them saying as they walked away.

In his mind, he couldn't help but wonder why they hadn't asked what he was selling or why he was selling it. The two of them just continued along the sidewalk.

That's okay, Cassius thought, as he inhaled the fresh morning air and looked around. The neighborhood looked as beautiful as ever.

A few minutes later, another lady, much younger, came running down the sidewalk a couple blocks away. Cassius straightened himself in his chair, and this time repositioned the large jar of lemonade right on the edge of the table.

He turned his gaze in her direction, awaiting her approach, but to his dismay, she turned, touched the stop sign at the corner of the intersection, and ran in the opposite direction. When she did this he let out a deep sigh—his second potential customer had now gotten away.

As he watched her disappear into the distance, Mr. Hyde's garage door opened, and inch by inch the man's body came into the beaming morning light. In his right hand he held a large bottle of water, and in his left he loosely gripped his lawnmower. As soon as he saw Cassius he held out a hand and waved, then walked in his direction.

"Cassius, our football star. What do we have here?" he said. Mr. Hyde had been retired for some years now, and on his face were heavy wrinkles, and in his hair only tiny streaks of brown remained. The man walked gingerly for his age.

Cassius cleared his throat for his elevator pitch.

"By golly, if I wasn't mistaken it looks like you're selling some lemonade," Mr. Hyde said.

"Yes, Mr. Hyde, some lemonade. It's pretty good too. Would you like to try some?" Cassius responded.

Mr. Hyde looked down, then raised his water bottle to his mouth and took a sip. He smacked his lips together. "Well," he began, "I'm sure whatever you're raising money for is for a good cause. I'm okay on the lemonade, but here, take this." Mr. Hyde reached into his pocket and handed Cassius a crisp twenty-dollar bill.

The young boy's eyes lit up with excitement. Though he

hadn't purchased any lemonade, someone had decided to give him a portion of their hard-earned money, and it felt good. "Thanks, Mr. Hyde! This means a lot to me. I'm raising money so my team can play on the Blue!"

"How much more do you have to go?" Mr. Hyde asked.

Cassius looked down at the twenty-dollar bill as if it were a foreign object. "Uh..." He eased out the creases with his hands.

Mr. Hyde quickly interjected. "Cassius! You should always know the state of your cash. You're a businessman, aren't you?"

"I think I am, Mr. Hyde."

"You think? How can a businessman not know the state of his investments? Because that's what you're doing, Cassius. You're investing. You invest your time, energy, and resources into something you hope will make you a profit. That's what investing is. And to do that effectively, you have to manage your cash. Cash is king."

Mr. Hyde walked away, back to his garage to use the lawnmower. His words still rang in Cassius's ears. Cash is king, cash is king. Cash is king. Cassius heard him, but yet at the same time he didn't really know what the words meant.

On Cassius went, watching cars drive by and people walk in his neighborhood then continue along their way. It even happened with the neighbors he knew, the ones he expected to buy. Why were the people in his neighborhood who had loved him so much before, people who had given him gifts on birthdays or had contributed to past team fundraising efforts, now not willing to support his lemonade business? Perhaps he wasn't running his business efficiently? Better yet, perhaps he wasn't managing his cash effectively as Mr. Hyde had said? What does that even mean? he thought to himself.

He was now faced with a great dilemma: he was eighty dollars short of his overall goal, and most of the people in his neighborhood who he thought would purchase a glass of lemonade had already passed by. It would only be a matter of time before the sun would set and Cassius would be forced to pack things up. He didn't have a plan B, so the thought of not reaching his goal—and of failing in his first business—scared him.

CHAPTER 11

"How are things going, son?" Mr. King asked. He had just finished doing some yard work in the backyard, and was now getting ready to weed eat the front.

"Fine," Cassius responded, a hint of dejection in his voice. Mr. King eyed his son up and down, then looked over the entire lemonade stand set up before him.

"How much?" Mr. King asked.

"Five dollars."

Mr. King's eyes widened. "Five dollars? How do you figure?"

Cassius simply shrugged. It was a price that sounded good to him, and he had plastered it all over the table halfway through the day so those near and far could see it.

"Son," Mr. King began, "don't you think that's a little high? For just a cup of lemonade?"

Mr. King reached into his pocket and removed from it a crisp five-dollar bill. He handed it to Cassius, who beamed ear to ear. He poured his dad a cup and handed it to him, which Mr. King slowly drank.

"Not bad," Mr. King said, smacking his lips. "Just the right amount of sugar. Is this your mother's recipe?"

"No. This is my own! I know just the right amount of sugar to put in each time. When Mom makes it, she doesn't ever put in the right amount."

"So this is your very own special recipe. That's pretty cool, Cassius."

"Thanks, Dad. I wish the others in the neighborhood would think so too, and buy a cup."

"Well how are you managing your cash? How are you using the cash you have right now to work for you to get you to more customers?" Mr. King asked.

Cassius was silent, thinking about what Mr. Hyde had told him earlier. Maybe there was something to what he had said. Perhaps cash was king.

"You know, Mr. Hyde came by and said the same thing, and he gave me twenty dollars. But I don't get it—how am I supposed to manage my cash? What can I do to use the cash I have to sell more lemonade?"

Cassius was now willing to hear his dad's advice. The day was almost over, and he was well short of his goal. He thought he had done everything right in order to run a successful lemonade stand, but the customers were not flowing in like he had expected.

"Do you remember Mr. Jamison? The one who lives down that way?"

"Yeah, Dad, the guy that works with you?"

Mr. King nodded.

"Yep, he would be a great resource for you to connect with. He can help you do just that—manage your cash and help you make the most of it so you can make your business better."

"Oh really?" Cassius asked, surprised. He had never heard Mr. Jamison utter a single word. "He works with you, right?"

"Right. He and I are partners—I cover the lending side of things, and he covers what we call cash management. He knows his stuff, inside and out, and he runs a few businesses of his own on the side too. I think he could really help you, son."

Cassius sat there, contemplating the idea of banging on Mr. Jamison's door, asking for advice on how to save his lemonade stand. He only had one more weekend before the funds were due, and he didn't have much time to waste.

"I guess I'll give it a shot, Dad. If you think I should."

"I think you should, son. Even if he isn't able to help you, what you'll learn from him will help you in the future. But I think he'll be able to lead you in the right direction." Mr. King walked back to the sidewalk, looking for little tiny weeds to trim near the edge of his lawn.

The sun had dipped so low that it was now partially hidden behind some low-hanging clouds. Cassius looked around the neighborhood—there wasn't a single person outside. He decided that his next move would be to regroup and go to Mr. Jamison for help, per his father's advice.

*

Ding, dong. Ding, dong. Ding, dong.

Cassius rang the doorbell and took a step back. Inside, he heard the sound of a dog barking.

“I got it, I got it. Settle down,” a voice inside called out. The dog continued its barking.

There was a twist of the lock and the door swung open. Mr. Jamison stood in the doorway, wearing a comfortable set of jogging sweats and a black fitted cap.

“Can I help you?” he asked.

“Hi, my name is Cassius King, I live down the way over there. Mr. King is my dad.”

“I know who you are. Your dad and I work together. How are you? How’s the football season going? Still undefeated?”

“Season is going great, Mr. Jamison. We finished the year undefeated. Third year in a row.”

“That’s fantastic. Your dad tells me your dream is to one day play on the Blue?”

“Yeah, and go to a BCS game, a national championship,” Cassius responded, glowing with pride.

“Well, I have no doubt you will do that.”

“Thanks, Mr. Jamison. Maybe I should tell you why I’m here.”

“Ahh, why you’re here. Right. What brings you to my door this evening?”

“Well, I’m here because I do have an opportunity to play on the Blue. Because my team finished undefeated, we got the chance to play in the regional tournament in Boise. But in order to go, we each have to raise a hundred dollars.”

“Very cool. So what are you going to do?” Mr. Jamison asked.

“Well, I was driving home with my mom the other day,

and while looking out of my window, I saw some kids running a lemonade stand. They had about five or six people in line waiting. So I figured that would be something that I could do too, especially since I already have the mix for it."

"So you're an entrepreneur? That's a big leap, Cassius."

"What's an entrepreneur?" Cassius asked.

"An entrepreneur is someone who takes on the risk to start a new business by providing goods and services, usually for profit. Like in your case."

"Ohh. So a businessman. My dad works with a lot of those. I've never thought about it, or asked him about his job. I wonder why he sent me to you?" Cassius asked.

"Yes, a businessman. But entrepreneurs can have their hands in many things, and usually they're pretty busy. Your dad probably sent you my way because I help entrepreneurs, too. But I do it in a different way."

"You're right about that, Mr. Jamison. I must be an entrepreneur, because I've been busy all day long. I started this morning before the sun came up, and if it weren't for me coming here, I'd still be sitting out there hoping for some people to come by to buy some lemonade."

"You said you have to raise a hundred dollars?"

"That's right."

"And how much have you raised so far?" Mr. Jamison asked.

"Twenty-five."

"Not bad for a day's work."

"But it all came from just two people. And I don't have

a lot of time. I only have one more week before the money is due."

"I see. So what are you going to do?"

"Well," Cassius began, "that's why I'm here, I guess. You're supposed to be able to teach me what you know about running a business, or entrepreneurship, that will help me sell more lemonade and make more money so I can play on the Blue."

"It's not as easy as it seems. I work in a department called cash management, and my goal for the entrepreneurs I work with is to help them streamline their cash flow so they can make the most out of their working capital."

Cassius stood there, head cocked to the side, staring at Mr. Jamison as if he'd just spoken a foreign language. The two of them stood in silence, Cassius searching for a few words to answer in response. Before he could speak again, Mr. Jamison interjected.

"Those are just some big words that simply mean that I'm the guy that helps you be as efficient as possible in managing your money. Does that make sense?"

A look of assurance washed over Cassius's face. The word efficiency made a bell go off in his mind.

"Efficiency. My dad uses that word all the time. He always tells me that a quarterback's job isn't really to be the most flashy or the most flamboyant, but it's to simply be efficient."

"Interesting. Very cool. You know, I'm watching a replay of one of my favorite Boise State games of all time. Do you remember the Fiesta Bowl win in 2007 against the Oklahoma Sooners?"

"Umm…"

"What? Unacceptable. That's where we'll start. Did you know that cash management in a lot of ways is like the game of football?"

"Is it?"

"I think it is. And that's how you'll learn about it. But before we begin, you have to promise me one thing."

"What's that, Mr. Jamison?"

"That you'll give me everything you've got. That you'll leave it all on the field when learning this stuff."

"You got it. Scout's honor."

"What does that mean?"

"It means you have my word." Cassius laughed.

"Great! See, we can both learn from each other. Well, come on in. I've got the game playing on replay on the television. Don't worry about the dog, he won't bite."

Mr. Jamison led the way into the house and into his living room, where the replay of the 2007 Boise State Fiesta Bowl was already playing. Cassius followed anxiously behind.

CHAPTER 12

"There are six key components to the game of football, not three, like most people think. Most people believe that there is only offense, defense, and special teams. While that's true, they often forget that the game isn't only won or lost on the field, but in preparation and prior to the field. In addition to offense, defense, and special teams, there is also film study, strength and conditioning, and practice. These six phases encompass the entire world of football. Without either, the game wouldn't be complete. Are you following me?"

On the television screen, Boise State quarterback Jared Zabransky motioned the fullback to his right side, followed by the tight end who had been lined up off the ball on the left side. He hiked the ball and dropped back deep in the pocket, faking a handoff to the running back, then taking his eyes downfield. The play action worked, and he sent a blazing dart all the way downfield to a wide open receiver who easily walked into the end zone. Six – zero, Broncos. Mr. Jamison's dog barked in excitement.

"Wow, did you see that, Mr. Jamison?" Cassius did all he could to contain his excitement. "Yep, I'm following you all right. That play must have taken a lot of practice!"

"Yes, it did, Cassius. I'm glad you're following me. Now, in the same way, every entrepreneur must successfully navigate six different areas if he too will succeed in effectively managing the day to day operations of his business. Those six areas are collections, disbursements, capital management, risk management, employee management, and information reporting. Without the effective management of these six areas, it becomes impossible to win on the field. Still following?"

"Mr. Jamison, that's a lot to take in. But like I promised, I'm here to learn as much as I can."

"That's the right attitude, Cassius. In cash management, the collections part of your business is like the offense. In other words, when you operate your collections efficiently, it helps you score points, or bring money in. Remember this about collections—an effective and efficient collections operation streamlines and centralizes your accounts receivable processes. In other words, it will help you shorten the time it takes you to get money from your customers after they purchase your lemonade, and into the bank so you can use it. Maybe to buy more materials or to pay yourself as well. Or, it could be saved and used at a later date, but we'll get to that later."

Mr. Jamison's dog barked again. With ten minutes to go in the second quarter of the game, the opposing team's quarterback dropped back and rolled to his left from the shotgun position, turned his body downfield, and threw a high arching ball into the endzone toward his receiver. A Boise State defensive back jumped in front of the ball and pulled down the interception, preventing the opposing team from tying up the game. Both Mr. Jamison and Cassius turned to watch the action as the crowd erupted in excitement following the prevented touchdown.

"What a play, what a play indeed," Mr. Jamison commented, shaking his head. "When the defense is clicking on all cylinders, meaning they are all on the same page, they take control of the game, they initiate things, rather than simply standing by and waiting for things to happen. I like to think of this in the same way an entrepreneur would handle disbursements. A proper disbursements operation means that the entrepreneur is initiating payments conveniently and efficiently. When an entrepreneur is efficient with his disbursements, he is able to save time by correctly managing the types of payments he initiates. In the same way, the defense can initiate turnovers—fumble recoveries, interceptions, fourth-down stops—that can transform a game in a heartbeat and halt the other team's momentum. Now let me ask you this, Cassius: How does your business handle collections and disbursements?"

Cassius sat there, staring at the television set. He hadn't really thought about how he would handle the money upon bringing it into his possession or selling a cup of lemonade, so Mr. Jamison's question caught him off guard.

"Well," he began. "I figure when I sell something, I'll just keep it in my pocket, or in the safe that my parents got me. Then when I raise enough, I'll take it out and turn it in." Cassius shrugged—it was all he could think of to say.

"I see. So what happens if you run out of lemonade, and you have the money locked away in a safe? What happens if you sell so much lemonade that your pockets get full?" Mr.

Jamison asked.

"Hmm... I guess I never thought about it in that much detail. What should I do to make sure I don't have any issues collecting or disbursing my money?"

"My job is to ask the right questions, and give you enough information so that you can think about it and come to your own conclusions as an entrepreneur. I rarely ever sit down and tell the people I work with exactly what to do. If you think about it, you'll come up with some ideas."

The Boise State quarterback dropped back and rolled to his right, evading a few defenders in the process. At the last minute, after being forced to step up into the pocket, he found a receiver to the far right of the field, and he threw a laser ball toward the sideline. The wide receiver caught the pass, turned to the inside, shook off a tackler, and darted toward the end zone. The crowd erupted as he ran to outpace the three defenders chasing him to make it for a touchdown. With all three looming close, he dove at the last second toward the near pylon and extended the ball, crossing the endzone.

"Collections," Cassius repeated, now with more understanding.

"Efficient collections. Very efficient," Mr. Jamison repeated, smiling, proud that Cassius was catching on.

"Are you ready to learn about capital management? The third of six that are extremely important in effective cash management?"

"I'm as ready as I'll ever be."

"Great. Let's watch more of the game, and I'll tell you

more about that in the second half."

After the touchdown, Boise State was now on top by eleven, with thirty-three seconds left to go in the half. After the kickoff, with twelve seconds remaining, the opposing team decided to go with a run up the middle, using their star running back, but the play was stopped behind the line.

CHAPTER 13

During the halftime performance, Mr. Jamison went to the kitchen and dished out some apple pie and ice cream. Cassius stayed in the living room area, looking at the pictures, occasionally glancing at the television. Mr. Jamison's Labrador retriever was sitting next to the sofa, head on his paws, nearly falling asleep. After a few minutes, Mr. Jamison returned, right on time for the start of the second half. He placed the dessert on the coffee table, sat down, and kicked his feet up on the island.

"Capital management, that's when we get to the good stuff," he began. "Most people don't see it as being very important, but by golly, it is one of the most important things. Now, let me get technical with you. But before I do that, what aspect of the game do you feel capital management most closely represents? Just take a guess."

Cassius had no idea, but he decided to go ahead and give a wild shot in the dark. They had already discussed offense and defense, so he figured he may have a shot if he said special teams.

"Special teams?" he asked.

"Is that a question or a statement?" Mr. Jamison responded.

"Um, both. I guess." Cassius folded his arms, nervous.

"Well, you're right. I see capital management just like I see special teams."

The teams had now taken the field and Boise State was kicking off to the opponent. The eleven men for the Broncos lined up on the line, and took off in unison with the kicker before he booted it high and deep, landing in the end zone and bouncing out of bounds for a touchback.

"When cash is truly king and managed as such, an entrepreneur makes his extra funds work smarter to meet his investment guidelines and business needs. He might take his money and put it into an account that can earn him interest, or reduce any expenses that he owes by using the money to pay it down. Or he may invest the money somewhere else. Maybe use it to buy something else that might make him money or start another business. The possibilities are endless."

Cassius was confused as to how special teams were in any way related to the description of capital management Mr. Jamison gave. "I don't get it," he finally blurted out. "Can you explain what you mean?"

"Of course. Special teams is a game of inches. It's about field position for the offense, or defense. Usually, whoever wins the special teams battle is the one who wins the game. Most people get so caught up with offense and defense that special teams become an afterthought, and they lose precious inches in field position. In the same way, if an entrepreneur loses sight of the money he has sitting in his possession, forgetting that it can be incrementally used for something that can set him up to capitalize on more business opportunities, then he too will lose out on precious 'field position' that can be gained by using his money effectively."

As the two watched the beginning of the second half, the game remained tight as the two top ten teams battled back and forth, fighting to gain the momentum. The ensuing action was filled with both hard offense and defense on both sides, and it seemed that the stalemate would last for some time, until an interception by Boise State's talented safety and punt returner led to another touchdown. But then, it was out of the formation on first and ten with eight minutes to go in the third quarter that the opposing quarterback dropped back into the pocket from his own twenty-five-yard line, turned to his left, then fired a ball to his wide receiver breaking on an out, only to find the safety waiting there for the interception and the score.

Boise State twenty-eight, their opponent ten.

As the action continued, it became clear that Boise State's opponent, the group of five powerhouse, would need to do something special to overcome the large deficit that they had mounted up against themselves. That moment came at about five minutes left to play in the third quarter, on a special teams play of all things. Cassius and Mr. Jamison watched the game as they ate their dessert, taking in the action. Mr. Jamison had purposely held off discussing any more about cash management, because he knew the coming play would encapsulate everything that he had tried to explain to Cassius about special teams.

It seemed like a routine play, one where the punter for the

opposing team received the snap for the punt and proceeded to boot it high into the sky for the Boise State punt returner to receive it. With the ball deep into their territory, and the opposing team racing toward him, the Bronco stepped to the side and let the ball bounce, hoping it would drop into the end zone for a touchback. Against their luck, the ball took an awkward bounce away from the endzone and in the opposite direction clipping the legs of a Boise State player. Their opponents recovered. Cassius, who had never seen the play before, now thought about what had transpired in light of what Mr. Jamison had told him about special teams. He glanced over at Mr. Jamison, who was licking his spoon, saying nothing. Two plays later, a handoff was made toward the left side and Boise State's opponent picked up a score off an eight-yard run. Finally, Mr. Jamison turned toward Cassius.

"Special teams," Cassius stated, beating Mr. Jones to the punch.

"Special teams indeed. A game of inches," Mr. Jamison responded.

The band fired off their fight song, and in a blink of an eye it was as if the Broncos opponents had been given new life. Cassius took his mind back to how both special teams and cash management related. He recalled Mr. Jamison's exact words:

"Special teams is a game of inches. It's about field position for the offense, or defense. Usually, whoever wins the special teams battle is the one who wins the game. Most people get so caught up with offense and defense that special teams become an afterthought, and they lose precious inches in field position.

In the same way, if an entrepreneur loses sight of the money he has sitting in his possession, forgetting that it can be incrementally used for something that can set him up to capitalize on more business opportunities, then he too will lose out on precious 'field position' that can be gained by using his money effectively." Cassius was able to recite what Mr. Jamison had said word for word.

"Very good," Mr. Jamison nodded in approval. "You remembered!"

CHAPTER 14

After the big special teams play and another field goal by Boise State's daunting opponent, the Broncos were now up just eight with fourteen minutes to go in the fourth quarter. The color analysts, as they'd done each and every game, fired off stats and storylines about both teams, engaging the audience around the world. One of those storylines included Boise State's durable, reliable running back, who had become known around college football as one of the toughest running backs to ever put on the blue and orange uniform.

A handoff on second and five up the right side to him led to a first down, and the announcers took the opportunity to jump into one of those storylines before another Boise State timeout and commercial break.

"To finish up the story about Ian Johnson being tough, he broke his ribs, punctured his lungs, and stayed in the game, spent five nights in a hospital in San Jose…"

"Wow," Cassius said. "Broken ribs? Punctured lungs? He's gotta be tough to endure that! I've never had anything like that happen to me."

"You're one of the lucky ones," Mr. Jamison responded. "Football is a brutal sport, and not many people can step away from the game without getting injured." Mr. Jamison went to a bookcase where several hundred books were packed away. Cassius watched as Mr. Jamison scanned the case of books, finally reaching for one. He looked it over for a second before turning and handing the book to Cassius. Cassius looked over its inscription.

"Exercise Injury and Rehabilitation." Cassius read it aloud, paying close attention to pronounce each word to the best of his ability.

"That's right," Mr. Jamison responded, plopping back into his seat. "This book right here is an athlete's dream. And it will help me explain another aspect of the effective management of your cash as an entrepreneur and savvy business owner."

"What does savvy mean?" Cassius asked.

"Savvy means you make good decisions. So if you are a savvy entrepreneur, it means you make great decisions as a business owner, usually leading to profit."

"Got it. So how can this help me run my business?"

"Let me first define risk and risk management as it relates to entrepreneurship, and cash management specifically. Effective risk management as an entrepreneur means you deploy resources, strategies, and tactics to help reduce your companies exposure to fraud and losses. Imagine if someone came by and took your hard-earned money from you, whether that be directly from your pocket, your piggy bank, or even a bank account. What would that be like?"

Cassius frowned. "Mr. Jamison, I'm too old to have a piggy bank. Those are for children."

"My apologies, Cassius. Yes, you are too old to have a piggy bank. So do you have a bank account?"

"No. But I've thought about opening one."

"As you should. And when you do, risk management is something you should be aware of and be spending a great deal of time thinking about."

"Okay, I'll remember that. But you still haven't explained to me how that relates to football, and specifically this book?"

"Let me ask you this: What would be the impact on Boise State if they lost Ian Johnson for a few games? What would be the impact to your team if they were to have lost you for a few games due to injury?"

Cassius sat there, thinking, trying his best to put the pieces together in his mind.

"That would be a pretty big loss. Our backup quarterback is Bones, and if Bones is at quarterback, we only have a handful of other receivers."

"Interesting. I don't know who Bones is, but it sounds like things would be shaken up quite a bit if you were out. You may be as worse off as Boise State would be without their star running back. Yeah, they could survive, but the impact to the team as a whole would be huge. And that, Cassius, is where this book comes in. In order to help reduce your company's—or your team's—exposure to losses, whether that be through a loss of money or through injuries, you need to make sure you focus on managing your risk. That's what will keep you in the game for the long haul."

Cassius nodded once more as he thumbed through the book. The pages contained all sorts of pictures related to athletes, and showed them doing things like stretching, running, working with athletic trainers, and even sitting in cold tubs and ice baths, something Cassius had never done and never planned to do, because he hated the cold. As he flipped through the pages, Mr. Jamison continued.

"When I was a youngster just like you, I ended up breaking my wrist in pee-wee football. I was a quarterback, too."

"You were?"

"Yes I was. It took me about eight weeks to recover, but still to this day I can't bend my wrist like I should."

"That bad of a break, huh?" Cassius asked.

"Yes and no. I fractured it in a place where the likelihood of refracture is high. Very high. And when I went back with a cast, I ended up rebreaking it somehow, and it set me back a few weeks."

"I see."

"But my point is that I clearly remember the doctors advising my dad and me that in order for me to avoid a rebreak of the wrist, I would need to make sure I managed the risk as effectively as possible. Those words never left me. And so I'll advise you the same way: With your lemonade stand you're going to run into quite a bit of risk—the most important one being the risk of losing your money before you get to one hundred dollars. You need to manage that risk effectively."

Cassius thought hard about Mr. Jamison's words, then about his own lemonade business. He figured he may need to devise a new plan on how he would keep track of his money, other than just stuffing it away in his pocket.

The risk is too high, he thought.

CHAPTER 15

It was late into the evening. Cassius and Mr. Jamison still remained fixated on the television, especially now that the game had been tied following Boise State's opponent's score and the subsequent two-point conversion as the equalizer. With a minute twenty-six in the fourth quarter to play, it was clear the game was going to come down to the wire. Even though Mr. Jamison knew the outcome, he was as glued to the television as if it were happening live. Both were on the edge of their seats, and even Mr. Jamison's dog was up on all fours, wagging his tail, watching every second of the game.

With two timeouts left to play in the game, the Boise State quarterback dropped back from the twenty-five-yard line and threw a laser ball toward the left sideline, hoping to connect with his wide receiver who looked to be breaking on an out route. The two were not in tandem, and the receiver kept running downfield. The defender, seeing the ball thrown, jumped in front of the ball and intercepted it, walking down the tightrope of the sideline for the touchdown. The extra point went straight down the upright, and with just one minute left to play, Boise State found themselves with their backs against the wall, unable to respond to their opponent's twenty-five unanswered points, after previously having complete control of the momentum of the game.

After the review of the play by the referees was announced, confirming that the defender did not step out of bounds, Mr. Jamison reached for the remote and held it toward the television with his hand. At the very moment the opponent's kicker was to connect with the ball on the kickoff, he hit the pause button, freezing the frame on the television.

Silence.

Mr. Jamison's dog froze in his tracks, tail stopped, and began whelping at the television. Cassius, unsure of what he was doing, held his gaze toward the television, waiting for whatever would come next. Seconds passed and still there was no movement by Mr. Jamison, only silence.

Slowly, after what seemed like an eternity, he lowered his hand and set the remote control on the center table. He folded his arms and rubbed his chin. "So what now?" he asked, still facing the television.

Young Cassius was oblivious as to how to respond.

"So what now?" he repeated, with the same, even tone.

"I don't know, Mr. Jamison. But I'm guessing there's another lesson here, right?" Cassius responded.

"Tell me what you see."

"What?"

"You play quarterback, right? And I'm sure you've been in this situation before, right? Walk me through what's going on in your head, if you were leading this team."

Cassius took a deep breath, and with eyes squinted, tried to place himself in the Boise State quarterback's shoes. He had been in a similar position in his last game, when he had to lead his team to the comeback victory. He tried his best to remember everything he'd observed during that game in the final minutes when it came down to the wire.

"Well, the first thing I notice is that I have a minute and two seconds left on the clock to try and score. So we are going to have to move fast down the field. Oh yeah, and I have two timeouts as well, so we may not need to just throw the ball deep, we have time."

Mr. Jamison nodded in approval. "Great, what else?"

"We're down seven points and we need a touchdown. Umm. What else is there?"

Mr. Jamison lifted the remote control and unpaused it, and the two watched as the ball was caught by the Boise State returner and returned to the twenty-two-yard line. The Boise State offense hustled onto the field, as the announcers informed those watching of the new college football rule that started the clock deep into the game once the chains were set. The Boise State offense got set in their formation, but before they could snap the football, Mr. Jamison pushed pause on the remote again.

"Now what do you see?" he asked.

"Well, my dad taught me that in these scenarios, I should always read the defensive backs. It looks like they're playing pretty far off, so I have some time to get the ball off."

"Long way before a touchdown though, right?" Mr. Jamison asked.

"Right. But we have two timeouts, remember?"

"I remember."

Mr. Jamison unpaused the game and the two watched as the Boise State quarterback dropped deep into the pocket, worked to the left, then found an open receiver in the middle of the field. The receiver caught the ball and darted up field for more yardage before being tackled at the forty-three-yard line—a gain of thirty-six. Rather than call a timeout, the Boise State team hustled to the line to get off another play, and perhaps catch the defense off guard. The quarterback hiked the ball, dropped back, but this time was met by a swarm of defenders who wrestled him down for the sack. The Broncos called one of their two remaining timeouts. Then, for the third time, Mr. Jamison hit the pause button on the remote.

"Nail biter, huh?" Mr. Jamison asked.

"Super nail biter," Cassius agreed.

"What do you think the key is to winning when the game is on the line?" It was another deep question.

Cassius paused, thinking back to his own team and their season, the game they had just won, and some of his dad's advice. "Playing smart. My dad always says that the smartest team under pressure will win."

"Interesting," Mr. Jamison responded. "I'm going to elaborate on that, if you don't mind. I believe the key to winning in crunch time has a lot to do with being the smartest team under pressure, yes, but the key to being the smartest team is having information and what you do with the information you have. Which leads me to my next point: Information reporting is one of the critical keys to effective cash management."

CHAPTER 16

Mr. Jamison began his teaching again. "In the same way you as the quarterback must effectively read the defense and the situation when your team is in deep down into crunch time, a savvy entrepreneur must also be aware of the situation when it comes down to crunch time in his business. Maybe you might expand your business offering, and instead of having one account under Cassius's Lemonade, you end up having two, and provide some other offering to your customers. If this happens, you'd need a way to look at both accounts to see how much money you have in them, and the detail behind what made up that cash balance. It would be important for you to know how much money you have at all times, right? So you can know exactly how close you are to getting to the hundred dollars, correct?"

"Correct. The faster I can get there, the better, so it would help to be able to see how much I have each day. But there's just one problem…"

"What's that?" Mr. Jamison asked, curious.

"Well," Cassius began, "my parents won't let me use the internet. And it's on the internet, right?"

"Well, yes, that's right. And that may not be a bad thing, Cassius. For a business owner like yourself, the internet could be a powerful tool, but in the world of cash management, there are other ways for you to know your cash balance at any particular time. You can choose to receive alerts on your account, if you create one, via phone, through text."

"Well, Mr. Jamison, it would probably help if I had a phone first, as well."

"In due time! You may need to make due for now without some of the benefits of information reporting, but down the road, just know it's something that could really help your business."

"Down the road…" Cassius voice tapered off as he spoke. "I'm not so sure I want to keep on being a business owner after all I've been through today, and now all of this…"

Mr. Jamison laughed. "It's not as easy as it looks, is it?"

"Not one bit. It's making my head spin, Mr. Jamison."

Mr. Jamison laughed, then turned toward the television and unpaused it.

"You know," Mr. Jamison began, "being a business owner, a savvy business owner, at that, should be fun. Managing your cash effectively should be even more fun."

"Really? Seems like a lot of work just to make money."

"What did you expect? For it to be easy?" Mr. Jamison replied.

"Well, yes. And no. I just didn't think that there would be so many little details to worry about. You know?"

"I know. A lot of the people I work with say the same thing. But I can tell you, without a doubt, that there is one thing that will make things a lot more fun."

Cassius waited, expecting for Mr. Jamison to divulge exactly what that thing was. Instead, he kept quiet, fixing his eyes on the football game.

Cassius did the same, hoping that Mr. Jamison would do just as he had done before—let a few key moments of the game go by, then explain to him exactly how it related to his lemonade stand, or Cassius's Lemonade, as he called it. Cassius liked the sound of that. So he sat up and moved toward the edge of his seat, excited for what would come next.

CHAPTER 17

"It's not the size of the dog in the fight, it's the size of the fight in the dog." Those were the magical words echoed by the Fiesta Bowl color commentator just as the extra point by the Boise State kicker Anthony Montgomery pierced through the uprights, kissing the back of the net and sending the game into overtime. It had been a few lackluster plays by the Broncos on their final drive going into the final seconds, and they found themselves facing a long fourth down and in need of a little Bronco magic, which they delivered. On a play they had likely practiced a thousand times, Jared Zabransky dropped back and threw a deep underneath pass to a crossing receiver, who took a few steps and lateraled to a man underneath, Jerard Rabb, who outraced the defenders to the endzone. Outrunning two defenders, Rabb crossed the goal line for a touchdown, evening the game in one of the wildest ends to a BCS football matchup that the world had ever seen.

"And that's how we do it on the Blue field every day in Boise in practice," another announcer said, fictitiously quoting head coach Chris Petersen as he slapped hands with an assistant. For Cassius, the end of regulation reminded him of his own end-of-season game, where they had scored a last-second touchdown to seal the win. Though the Broncos had not yet won, the energy he felt running through his veins was similar. A high camera pan showed the small sea of Boise fans in the stadium going wild, while the cheerleaders jumped up and down with uncontrollable excitement, waving their colorful pom poms high into the air.

"Overtime!" Mr. Jamison called out as he got up and walked into the kitchen. As Cassius watched the screen, he kept an eye on Mr. Jamison's dog. He was still sitting there, licking his paw. Cassius could hear some plates and utensils being moved around in the kitchen. Mr. Jamison was back in the fridge again.

"More dessert, Cassius?" Mr. Jamison called out. "Might as well, given we're headed to overtime." He laughed.

Cassius smiled, partly thinking about dessert, partly thinking about the game, but mainly thinking about the lesson.

As Mr. Jamison reentered the living room, two big bowls in hand, the game returned from a steady stream of commercials.

Anticipation filled the air as the announcers informed the television audience of the ground rules to be abided by during the playoff. Each team would be given one possession from their opponent's twenty-five-yard line, with the leader after those possessions being crowned the winner. If the game remained tied after that first possession, then the sequence would continue until one team led at the end of possession. The last rule would be the most daunting: After the second overtime, each team would be required to attempt a two-point conversion.

Cassius looked down into his bowl to see three scoops of vanilla caramel ice cream—his favorite. He dropped a large spoonful into his mouth, sinking deeper into the couch as his eyes rolled over. A taste of heaven, he thought. Mr. Jamison looked to be a bit more on edge, or excited for that matter, and he sat on the edge of his seat watching as the overtime play was to begin. It was as if he was seeing the action for the first time, and even more, it appeared to Cassius that he had forgotten about all of the lessons and was now solely focused on the action of the game.

The three captains from each side walked to the middle of the field for the coin toss. As they did this, Cassius looked over to Mr. Jamison, who was nodding as if to approve. The Broncos won the toss and elected to go on defense first—a strategic move that would position them well for the win if they were able to hold their opponent to a field goal first. The Oklahoma Sooners chose which end of the field they wanted to defend, and the action was on. Mr. Jamison reached for the remote as the Sooners took the field and turned up the volume a few notches.

It wasn't long before lighting struck for the Sooners—on the very first play of regulation, Paul Thompson handed the ball to their powerful and dynamic half back, Adrian Peterson, who scooted between the left tackles and up the sideline, avoiding all contact and doing a tiny skip into the endzone for a score. It seemed so easy that not even the announcers seemed surprised.

"Here we go," Mr. Jamison quipped as he picked up his

bowl of ice cream. "Are you paying attention?"

"Yes, Mr. Jamison, I am." Cassius was surprised at how easy the score had come.

After the extra point went straight through the uprights, it was the Broncos' turn to take the field to attempt to even the score in order to send the game into a second overtime. Jared Zabransky walked to the line of scrimmage and sent his fullback in motion. At the snap, a pitch was made to the half back, who typically lined up at wide receiver, but it was stuffed at the line of scrimmage.

Second down.

The Broncos again approached the line of scrimmage with composure. They were lined up in the shotgun position, three wide receivers and a half back to the left, with a tight end on the line of scrimmage to the right. Zabransky sent the third wide receiver into motion and snapped the ball. Rolling to his left, he spun around and found his tight end who had slipped back from the line of scrimmage and drilled him with the quick pass. Although the Broncos were able to secure a few good blocks downfield, it was no match for the mighty swarming defense of the Oklahoma Sooners. The Bronco was tackled for a tiny gain of two.

Third down.

"They'll have to change the way they are thinking. Different type of drive now that the first two downs have stalled," Mr. Jamison said, shaking his head. "What do you see, Cassius? What information are you pulling in based on the situation?"

Cassius scanned over all of the data available on the screen.

It was third down and long, seven to be exact, and nothing of the glitz and glamor that Boise State had done on the preceding plays had worked. They would be forced to throw the ball downfield.

"They gotta find a whole in the coverage, and get the ball downfield," Cassius said, taking his best guess as to what play was coming next.

The Broncos approached the line with two backs, but shifted, as was typical, into a new formation at the line of scrimmage. They were successful in getting the defense to shift with them into a new position as well. Upon the hike of the football, the Boise State quarterback dropped back into the pocket, and threaded a stinging dart of a pass straight into the middle of the field, finding a hole in the defense and connecting with his open tight end, who stumbled and bumbled inside the fifteen-yard line.

It was another Bronco first down.

"Good call. Way to read the information," Mr. Jamison said.

The Broncos could now breathe, as they now had another fresh set of downs to reach the end zone and tie the game. The next play, though slower to develop, was a hand off to a motioning receiver, Vinny Peretta, who cut up the field but was stopped for a tiny gain of two.

"It looks like his knee was down there, and we got away with one," Mr. Jamison stated emphatically. "That's usually the case in big games."

Cassius nodded silently as his eyes remained glued on the

action. He hadn't blinked in some time.

This time, on second down, the Broncos broke from the huddle and moved toward the line of scrimmage with more urgency. The quarterback snapped the football and handed it off to Ian Johnson who charged up the middle behind two pulling guards, finding a crease within the defense and picking up a gain that left the Broncos about a foot short of the first down. It was a perfect read by him to find the crease, and the run put him over a hundred yards on the ground for the day. It would now be a crucial third down. The Broncos would need to gain one yard on the play to pick up the first, and to gain a fresh set of downs to try and puncture the ball into the end zone.

With little hesitation, they broke the huddle and lined up in a running formation—twenty-three personnel with two tight ends and three backs in the back field. Once again they shifted their men before the play, getting the Sooners' defense to move as well. Zabransky hiked the football just before the defenders were able to get set, and handed it off again up the middle to Ian Johnson who was stuffed at the line and even let the ball loose just as he was going down. Cassius held his breath—it looked like the ball had come loose prior to him being down, but he wasn't sure.

"Disbursements!" he called out, almost instinctively.

Mr. Jamison smiled. "Or, just a close call."

The officials signaled to the head replay booth to have the play reviewed. After a few moments, the referees returned and confirmed the ruling on the field that the runner was down. Cassius let out a sigh of relief.

Fourth down. Two yards to go.

Everything, the entire Tostitos Fiesta Bowl Championship, would now come down to this next play. Mr. Jamison reached for the remote and froze the game. He took in a deep breath and smiled.

"What a game, huh?"

Cassius simply smiled in return, his eyes fixed on the paused screen. Mr. Jamison continued.

"Now, I know you may not be expecting this, but the last phase of effective cash management as a savvy business owner on the surface has nothing to do with cash—or even you for that matter."

Cassius instantly became confused. "What do you mean?"

"I mean that there's something that I want you to pay close attention to in the final moments of this game that will explain the most important lesson of all. It will explain what, in my experience, makes being a business owner and an entrepreneur so fun. Watch."

Mr. Jamison unpaused the screen, and the action continued.

On the fourth-down conversion, Vinny Perretta lined up in the back field next to the quarterback. A set of motions ensued and the latter moved to the running back's position in the shotgun, leaving Perretta as the signal caller to receive the ball from the center. A lift of his leg sent Jared Zabransky out wide to the left side, leaving just the converted wide receiver in the back field.

What are they doing? Cassius thought.

At the hike of the football, Perretta dashed to his right immediately, appearing as if he was going to tuck the football and run, but at the last minute, pulled up and through a looping pass to none other than the tight end, Derek Schouman, who had squeaked free and was making his way to the corner of the end zone. He had a step on the defender, and he pulled down the ball for the score.

Both Cassius and Mr. Jamison leaped from their seats with their hands raised.

"WOOOO!" Cassius yelled out. "That was sweet!"

"Oh yeah, a little Bronco magic, huh?" Mr. Jamison replied enthusiastically.

"On to another overtime," Cassius said as he leaned toward the edge of his seat.

"Not so fast." Mr. Jamison was now rubbing his hands together, seemingly champing at the bit.

As the Broncos briefly celebrated the play, running toward the sideline while the fans in the stadium jumped up and down with excitement, Charles Davis, the color commentator, chimed in.

"They're going to go for two guys. Listen, I'm telling you. When you're Cinderella, at a certain point, you don't keep sluggin' with the big guy. You're going to try and win the football game right now. That's what I'm telling you."

The announcer, knowing the spirit of the men in blue fighting against Goliath, believed that Boise State would go for two, to win it all. And as the Broncos looked to the sideline to receive the play, everyone watching could see that the announcer was right, as the offense remained on the field to attempt the two-point conversion. The offense once again approached the line with determined confidence in spite of the stakes. As they did so, the Oklahoma Sooners' head coach, Bob Stoops, signaled to the referee to give them a timeout, allowing for he and his staff to read the formation and get a jump on the coming play. It was a strategic move that would have likely been favorable to any other team. But the Broncos were different. Because of their constant shift and motion prior to the snap, no team all season could really get a jump on what exactly they were doing.

As the final play of the game inched closer, the cameras in the stadium panned to several different fans, some holding their hands up in prayer, others holding both hands together over their heads, then finally down to the opposing teams players, where some on the team knelt toward the field, anticipating the big finale.

In that moment, the announcers made defiant claims for the right for a team like Boise State to compete for a national championship, a claim for the underdog that never really got the respect it deserved. But in this moment, they had fought valiantly to the end of the game, they had weathered the highs and the lows and had fought their way back to now put them in a position to showcase their skills as the entire nation watched.

Cassius held his hands up in anticipation, slowly rocking back and forth, subconsciously. Mr. Jamison was standing erect, his foot resting on the coffee table where the empty dessert bowls sat, his arms folded across his chest. His stoicism held back his true emotions, though he had seen the game several times, the excitement of the grandness of the game whenever he watched it thrilled him.

This was it.

Jared Zabransky directed his teammates with a few hand signals as the team approached the line of scrimmage. They set themselves in a single back formation, with three receivers in bunch formation to the right side of the field. At the snap of the football, the inside receiver bubbled toward the sideline, raising his hands up to receive the screen pass. Zabransky darted back, completing his three-step drop and staring down his receiver to the right of the field. The Sooners swarmed in that direction with reckless abandon, trying to converge and stuff the play before it could even begin. Zabransky would have to fire a perfect dart to complete it, as the three receivers were completely blanketed.

Cassius held his breath, realizing that the Sooners had completely snuffed out the play. Mr. Jamison, to Cassius's surprise, started laughing, just as the ball was snapped.

Cassius soon found out why. The color commentator's voices exposed what was unfolding on the field.

"And Boise State for the win. They hand it off to Johnson! Boise State has won the Tostitos Fiesta Bowl! Can you believe it!"

It was a fake! Ian Johnson had stealthily been hanging behind the quarterback the entire time, waiting for him to pump fake to the sideline, but then dip the ball behind his back with his off throwing hand. Boise State's most durable back held the fake for just the right amount of time, only at the last minute darting toward his left, grabbing the football, and racing toward the end zone. Ryan Clady, the Broncos' All-American, powerful tackle, came screaming around the edge to lead the way, passing by another Bronco lineman who had successfully sealed the corner. By this time the Oklahoma Sooners had caught on, and tried to redirect themselves toward the other side of the field. But it was too late. Ian Johnson ran into the endzone, untouched, for the game-winning score. The play was executed to perfection.

And the crowd agreed—they went wild. And so did Cassius. The young boy almost flew out of his seat. Mr. Jamison stood there with a beaming smile across his face, as if to be acknowledging the beauty of what he had just seen. It had been some time since he had seen that magical ending unfold, and as he stood there he savored every moment, recollecting the very time he saw the game live on the television. Time had passed, but his memories hadn't.

"Ho-LY COW!" Cassius yelled out. "Did you see that?"

Mr. Jamison continued smiling. "Isn't that something? Perfect execution. But what else? What else, Cassius?" His tone became a bit more serious. With the excitement, Cassius had forgotten that there was still one final lesson to be learned.

"Uhhh. Winning? That's what makes the game fun, and business. Right?" he asked.

"Not so much, my friend. Winning is great, and it is a result of the team or a business owner playing a complete game. But it isn't the be all and end all. Sometimes a team may play well in all six areas of the game, and still come up short. So no, winning isn't it. What else can you think of?"

Cassius looked with laser-like focus at the television screen—the players celebrating joyously as they made their way around the field prior to the presentation of the trophy. As they gathered, the field announcer pulled aside Jared Zabransky to get his thoughts on the game. "It's unbelievable. These guys just kept believing and kept believing. And that shows where they got it, they got it right here. We just kept battling, from that last play of regulation to that play, it was unbelievable," he answered.

"Biggest win in the history of Boise State football, what about that final play, the fake without hesitation to go for two?" he asked.

"I mean we wanted to come out here and win, we weren't going to hold anything back. We've been practicing that play all season long. Actually it was our backup quarterback who put that extra fake in. And it was just. It worked out… We ran it against Idaho and it was good and we just held on to it until now."

Cassius could see Mr. Jamison peeking at him out of the corner of his eye. But Cassius was unable to put the dots together. So he sat there, watching as Ian Johnson proposed to his cheerleader girlfriend on national television and as the players hugged family members in the stands and took photo after photo at the center of the field. He sat there watching, as Mr. Jamison's dog wagged his tail, looking as if he were getting ready to jump into the television. It wasn't until the presentation of the trophy that Mr. Jamison spoke again. He pushed the pause button just as Coach Petersen lifted the golden football high into the air while exclaiming. "This one here is for the Bronco Nation!"

Mr. Jamison took a deep breath.

"Now, up until now clues have been dropping from the sky as to what the sixth key is, the thing I know for a fact will make business fun. Have you caught it yet?"

Before Cassius could answer, Mr. Jamison kept going, knowing for a fact that young Cassius hadn't yet caught the message.

"Listen carefully okay?" he said, turning his attention back to the screen and pushing play.

"Coach," the man conducting the interview began, "do you feel like you shocked the world tonight?"

"I tell you what, our guys fight and crawl and scratch and play as hard as anybody in the country, and when you do that you know you always got a chance. All the credit goes to these warriors out here."

"Let's be honest though, I don't think there's any more pages in that playbook. I mean that last one, that forced overtime, where did you come up with that?" the announcer asked.

"Well, I gotta tell you this," Coach Pete began. "The two backup QBs are the ones that have been calling for it all game long. And so there's a lot of credit that goes a lot of places and it starts with Taylor Tharpe and Bush Hamden as much as anybody for calling that play right there."

The crowd erupted with cheers as the announcer raised his

final question.

"Coach, obviously it means the world to Boise State and the western athletic conference, what does this mean to all the mid majors if you will out there?"

"Well, we're just so happy that the BCS people tweaked the system to give us a shot to get here, because when you get here you never know what can happen…like tonight."

"Coach, you're not necessarily stronger, or faster… you're just better. And you're also the 2007 Tostitos Fiesta Bowl Champions. Congratulations Coach."

"Thank you very much," Coach Petersen responded, as he again lifted the trophy ball high into the air as the crowd roared with cheers.

It was a fitting end to a prolific and exciting game, one filled with ups and downs, and lessons in between. But the final lesson had not yet been revealed. Curious, considering the game had ended, Cassius awaited for Mr. Jamison to continue.

What could be the final lesson?

*

A Break In the Action
Cash Management: A Seemingly Commoditized Business

When discussing cash management, at a high-level a banker is first and foremost engaging in a conversation regarding a business clients accounts payable and accounts receivable. As it relates to accounts payable, there is the invoice, the workflow, the actual payment and the subsequent reconciliation and posting back to the customers accounting or ERP (Enterprise Resource Planning) system. When having a conversation with any business owner, this structure and flow allows for the seasoned banker to start from a much broader sense, then dig down deeper as needed over the flow of the conversation. A great cash management officer will seek to learn, understand, and ask questions about everything concerning accounts payable upfront. How many employees do you have? Is your accounting department centralized or decentralized? He will request for the customer to explain everything to him or her in as great of detail as possible. A great cash advisor will seek validation that he, the banker, is hearing the right thing. A consequence of this is that it will assist the bank and the banker during the very crucial implementation process after a sale is made. A sophisticated cash management advisor understands how terrible things are when the file formats don't work, or the ERP or accounting system is not being fed data to correctly, et cetera. A failure to validate critical information is the seed that leads to problems and issues down the road.

As it relates to the discussion of invoicing, a great cash management adviser will ask you to explain in depth how you and your company are receiving any and all invoices. Is it via mail or email? If by mail, how are you getting from the mailroom to your workflow for appropriate approval? How many invoices are you receiving via mail versus email?

It is critical that both you and your bank dive deeper into your workflow. You have an invoice via paper, what happens next? Are you scanning them into a system to get approved? What is that system? Who has to approve those invoices prior to them being paid? How are you making those payments on those invoices? Are you using a credit card, ACH, paper check, or wire? Are you currently set up with a virtual card? And once these payments are being made how are you reconciling them payments back into your ERP or accounting system?

At first glance, these may seem like simple and high-level questions to be asking, but this just takes the cash management advisor beyond mere payments and into the seat of the business owner. Most cash management and treasury individuals are focused solely on the payment piece only, much to their detriment. I would go so far as to say that the majority of the competition in this space is focused on just that aspect. Why is this a problem? Because the officer is missing out on acting as a trusted advisor when solutions are available to assist the customer with each of these processes. In the final analysis, treasury is a commoditized business—price times volume as many people in the field would say. Every single bank on every single corner has credit cards, ACH, checks and wires, and because of it, the average banker merely aims to beat the price that another bank is offering. Perhaps there are a few little differences, such as reporting for wires where the details can be found in the previous day report on the online banking platform, but one must question whether the client is willing to even pay an additional amount for such a feature. So, again, the conversation historically and up until this time has been commoditized down to just price times volume and is usually solely focused on payment execution. Therefore it is critical that one focuses on a holistic approach to the entire accounts payable process.

To explain further, take for example a customer using a distributed commercial card, meaning that he or she uses physical cards for those employees working in the field or travelling from location to location. Let's say that the customer reaches out on a random day to the relationship manager because they have just heard that there is a new functionality that links their banking to their accounting system. The treasury officer arranges a sit down with the customer and at once begins a high level discussion regarding their payables process, after some brief introductions, of course. After their immediate needs are addressed, the officer asks a simple and general question: How are you using your commercial card today? This open-ended question invites the customer to open up. As the customer goes through his or her process, the advisor is immediately able to confirm that the customer's ERP system is a QuickBooks. They proceed to divulge that each of their employees with a distributed card is getting his or her statement from a staff employee who is going into another internal reporting software system called Harvest, and pulling every single credit card statement manually by hand, and depending on their particular mood on that given day, they are either printing them out and placing them on each card holders desk, or scanning them and sending them to the cardholder via email. What the client has just described is their workflow. As you can imagine, this can be a tedious and cumbersome process, especially considering the customer has over thirty card-holding employees.

That individual who has been given the statement then goes into Harvest to complete his or her expense report. They take the line item off of the statement and hand key them into Harvest, carefully coding each individual transaction to a project, hoping they are not missing the project code associated. It is explained that if they miss any code in Harvest, the company is left responsible because the system bills each of their clients.

The officer, likely surprised by the long and tedious process, asks how the company is handling the rest of their accounts payable using purchase card. The officer soon finds out that the customer is using a whole different program for their AP. The customer is using a third party where they are prefunding the card based on their anticipated receivables. Shocked, the cash management advisor now realizes that the bank for which he works does not have the whole of the companies payables business—costing them critical non-interest income revenue.

Upon regaining his composure, the officer asks how the company is doing all the distributed and purchase card reconciliation. The client states that they have nor workflow hierarchy approval process, so the accounting manager is manually keying from the workflow into the Harvest software. She is taking the employee expense reports and entering it manually into QuickBooks.

Through this basic scenario, you may be able to see that there is much room for automating the clients process by diving deeper into their entire workflow, rather than simply focusing solely on the payment portion.

When all is said and done, a seasoned cash management representative would seek to establish the following flow of discussion with a prospect or a business owner:

Accounts Payable Workflow:

1. Pre Questions:
   - How many employees do you have?
   - Are you centralized or decentralized?
   - What accounting/ERP system do you use?
2. Invoice (A/P):
   - Mail or email?
   - How many invoices?
   - How much time does it take to capture the invoice?
   - How many employees work in A/P?
   - How do you capture and store data?
3. Workflow:
   - Who must approve the invoices?
   - Are the approvers in the office or remote?
   - Any limits to what can be approved?
   - How much time does workflow take?
   - How do you handle expense reporting?
4. Payment:
   - Do you receive discounts or have terms with your suppliers?
   - What ways are you currently paying?
   - What are your volumes? Number of payments and size.
   - How often are payments being sent out?

5. Reconciliation:
    - How do you get data back into your accounting system?
    - Do you have any type of security for fraud prevention?

And the Accounts Receivable Workflow:

1. Invoice Statement (A/R)
    - Are you mailing or emailing invoices?
    - How many invoices are you sending?
    - How much time does it take to create an invoice?
    - Do you offer your customers terms?
    - How are you storing invoices?
    - How do you take payments?
2. Payment
    - How many payments are you receiving?
    - Are you accepting web payments/telephone/etc.
    - What are your volumes? Number of transactions/size of transactions/frequency
3. Cash Ap (Reconciliation)
    - How do you post back to your accounting system?
    - How are you reconciling check, credit card and cash payments?

An experienced cash advisor will seek to understand the

complexities of his customer or prospect's business by expanding beyond the traditional payments discussions and moving toward a more holistic approach as it relates to the movement of funds in and out of the client pr prospects business. As a business owner, employee, or entrepreneur, you should always be challenging your bankers to think beyond the commoditized payment piece of cash management and into the deeper waters of the ins and outs of your business. If your banker is not prepared to have these discussions, it may be time to reevaluate with which bank you do business, because it is likely that such a relationship is costing you both time and money.

EPILOGUE

Riding on the heels of watching the electrifying win by the Boise State Broncos, Cassius went to sleep that night with a sense of optimism about the success of his lemonade stand and his ability to raise the funds needed. He took another week to plan out everything he needed in detail to open up the stand for the second time, and raise the full one hundred dollars.

The following Saturday, he set his alarm early, for six in the morning, and rolled out of bed once it went off, just before the sunrise. This time, he thought, things will be different. He now understood the meaning behind the saying, "Cash is king."

He rumbled down the steep stairs and made his way into the kitchen, where he fumbled through the cupboards and pulled out some fresh ingredients he had purchased at the grocery store just a few days prior. Thanks to Mr. Jamison's advice, he had decided that the best place to keep the money was not in his pocket, but in an actual account at the bank. After registering his company, Cash Enterprises, he and Mr. King took an afternoon and together went down to the bank in which Mr. King worked and opened up a basic business checking account, which required no minimum deposit to get going. He took the debit card given to him as a part of the account opening and went off to the grocery store to get his ingredients and a few more supplies, taking advantage of a ten-dollar credit given for new accounts.

As he pulled them from the cupboard he checked the time on his watch—it would be just a few more minutes before the sun would fully rise and the neighbors and the community would start coming out to tend to their lawns. Cassius mixed up the ingredients and left the tasty, fresh lemonade on the counter as he ran into the garage to get the table and the chairs set up in his driveway. Using big blue and orange markers, reflective of his favorite Bronco team, he crafted out his company name and logo by hand on a large sheet of white cardboard that he had found in his garage, taping it to the front of the table. Then, after nearly forgetting, he ran back inside and grabbed the gift that his mother and father had gotten him the day after his time with Mr. Jamison. It was a small cash register that they'd given him that gave him a constant reading of the amount of money he had received.

As he got all of his ducks in order, he thought back to the lessons Mr. Jamison had taught him just a week before.

"Collections. Disbursements. Capital management. Risk management. Employee management. Information reporting," he whispered to himself. It was an entire new world that he had been exposed to, but given he could now see it in the same way as he saw his Boise State Broncos, he knew that in time, if he wanted to, he could become just as savvy as an entrepreneur managing his cash as he was as the quarterback for his team.

So there he was, the sun was now rising in the sky, neighbors were making their way into their yards, and Cassius was ready to serve them.

Well, almost.

There was that final lesson, the one which Mr. Jamison said was most important, the one that would make running his business both fun and entertaining. He hadn't thought about it before, but now as he sat there, it all make sense. He knew that all the parents likely had the money to afford to go to the regional tournament, but yet they were making all the kids raise the dollars themselves. It was an odd move, but in retrospect, he could now see why. It was the same reason why Boise State's then-head coach Chris Petersen chose to say what he said on the podium after the game, and why Jared Zabransky gave the response he did to the sideline reporter as the crowd roared with excitement.

He folded his arms, reflecting on all of it, just as a big blue van rolled up to the front of his driveway, and out popped several of his teammates: Kareem, Bones, and Rimar, who were each smiling from ear to ear.

"Hey Cassius!" They ran to his table, hands full. All three were holding in their hands a plate full of delicious sweets—pies, cookies, and cakes. Each one was separately wrapped and had a price tag on it and were to be sold with Cassius's ice cold lemonade.

Bones's mom, who had driven the boys over, winded down the passenger window and waived.

"Have fun boys! Go raise that money! Teamwork!" She

yelled. The four boys, so excited to be hanging out as good friends on a Saturday morning, failed to waive back. Instead, after slapping hands and giving high fives, they each set up their items, grabbed the big blue and orange pen, and began adding their own words to the sign.

Cookies – $1.00
Cakes – $1.00
Pies – $2.00

It turned out that Bones's mother was on to something, for it was the power of teamwork that Mr. Jamison wanted to teach the young Cassius. "If you want to fly high, fly alone, but if you want to fly far, fly together," he had explained to Cassius after they had finished watching Boise State pull off the miraculous win. Mr. Jamison had called it "employee management" as it related to cash management and his "cash is king" philosophy. "Employee management," he said, "provides key benefits that reward and helps to retain any savvy entrepreneur's employees." In other words, it is the care and recognition of one's workers that ultimately leads to their satisfaction with the company.

And now Cassius was beginning to put that to practice. As he had thought about his efforts the previous week to raise the money on his own, he realized he was miserable sitting out there all by himself, pushing to sell a product of his own making and design, rather than including and weaving in others along for the journey. It turned out that Mr. Jamison was exactly right, including others in on his venture, and sharing a piece of the pie so to speak while flying together was exactly what Cassius needed to shake things up and make things fun. That was the key to going far and having a good time.

*

The three boys had a great time that morning working together to sell the lemonade and baked goods to the community. Cassius and Rimar decided that they would go around the neighborhood and knock on doors to tell people about the lemonade stand and why they were trying to raise money, while Bones and Kareem stayed behind and manned the lemonade stand. The strategy worked, and soon upon returning from their door blitz, people from all across the neighborhood came walking by, many with their pets and spouses, and they stopped for a cup of lemonade and a baked treat. The boys' were ecstatic as they made each sale. Cassius carefully counted the money and distributed the change, putting the funds into the cash register and no longer into his pocket. By noon they had raised over $150, and they were soon running out of product. Cassius decided to run inside and tell Mr. and Mrs. King, who happily drove him to the supermarket to buy some more baked goods and ice for the lemonade. He kept track of the purchase, noting that it cost him twenty dollars. It was a good thing he did, because upon his return all of the baked goods and lemonade were gone.

"An old man came by and bought up everything," Bones

said. "When we told him we'd have to wait until you got back to get the change for his hundred-dollar bill, he just said keep it. Then the man left."

Cassius wondered who the man could have been. Either way, they were now so close to their goal of three hundred dollars, or one hundred dollars each. But it was now past the busy hour for people to be out and about tending to their lawns, and it didn't look as if anyone else would be coming by anytime soon.

"How much do we got left to raise?" Rimar asked.

Cassius popped open the cash register and counted out the money.

"About seventy," he said, a bit of dejection in his voice.

Bones let out a sigh. "What are we going to do?" he asked. "The money's due in a few days."

The three of them sat in silence. It was so quiet you could hear a pin drop.

"Well. I guess it just wasn't meant to be," Cassius said, sinking his head to his chest. "I guess we won't be making the trip after all."

Just as Cassius rose from his seat to begin leading the effort to pack up the stand and take it inside, he heard a car honking in the distance. All three boys looked down the street, and as the car came closer they saw that it was Bones's mother. It caught them by surprise, as the two boys were to be spending the night, and she was to pick them up the following day. But as she approached, they noticed she was not alone. In the car with her was Bones's dad, and Rimar's mom and dad in the back seat. As she rolled down the window, she waved—not at Cassius, Bones, or Rimar, but at Mr. and Mrs. King, who had just walked outside.

What could be going on? Were the boys in trouble? Seeing their parents all coming together caught them off guard.

Bones's mom parked the car and all four of them exited the vehicle and met the boys and Mr. and Mrs. King in the driveway. After some brief hellos and laughter they all turned to the group and Mr. King addressed them.

"We've been watching from the window, and you guys have done a great job working as a team," he began. "How much have you raised? Did you hit your goal?"

The three boys shook their heads no.

Bones's dad spoke up next. "Well how far off are you? It looks like you still have some items to sell." He pointed at a few of the baked goods.

"We need another seventy dollars, Dad," Bones replied.

The six adults looked at one another, then Mr. King motioned them together a few feet away from the table. They met in a group secretly for almost a full minute, as the boys waited patiently at the stand. Finally, they broke and came back to the table.

"Well," Mr. King began. "I have to say, son, I'm quite impressed with what you've done here. How did you do it, Cassius?"

"Cassius was smiling on the inside, for being complimented by his dad always felt good. He wiggled around in his seat, thinking of how he would explain how he came up with the idea. But just before he was to speak, he looked up and saw all eyes on him, and he looked to his left, where Rimar sat, and to his right, where Bones was sitting. He held his tongue just one more moment and thought back to his time with Mr. Jamison as they watched his favorite team pull off the improbable victory in the Tostitos Fiesta Bowl against the mighty Oklahoma Sooners.

"Well," he began. "The answer, Dad, is that I didn't do it. I couldn't do it." Cassius was fumbling for words.

"Explain, son," Mr. King encouraged him.

"Well I tried last week, and nothing went well. I didn't come close to raising the money. And it wasn't any fun. But now, with Bones and Rimar, we did really well, and we had a lot of fun."

Mrs. King's face lit up as she listened to her son speak. Mr. Gary, Bones's Dad, decided to chime in.

"Did you tell them about how your bake sale went last weekend, son?"

"No," Bones began. "I had a bake sale in my neighborhood last week, and I only made about forty bucks. And it wasn't any fun."

"What about you, Rimar?" his mother chimed in.

"Same. I only raised twenty in my neighborhood. And it was so hot I had to pack up early."

"So it looks like you all really needed each other to get the job done. And you raised almost the whole amount today. But what about together?"

The boys had forgotten up to this point that they had each

raised some of the money on their own the last weekend.

"Together, if you add the twenty-five you made, Cassius, and the forty and twenty the two of you made, you have well beyond your total."

The three boys looked at each other with amazement. They realized in that moment the power of teamwork and why flying together was so important. All along, it was the lesson Mr. King and the other coaches wanted them to learn. Yes, they could have paid the money for each of them to go on the trip—the money wasn't the issue. Mr. King and his staff wanted the boys to learn an important lesson, not merely about the power of handling one's cash effectively, but about the power of relying on friends, family, employees, and teammates to get a job done.

"Teamwork makes the dreamwork, huh guys?" Mr. King said.

The three boys, still processing the fact that they had accomplished their goal and would soon be playing on the Blue, nodded with big toothy grins plastered on their faces.

"Yeah, Dad!" Cassius exclaimed. "Yes it does."

The End

www.ingramcontent.com/pod-product-compliance
Ingram Content Group UK Ltd.
Pitfield, Milton Keynes, MK11 3LW, UK
UKHW042017290726
14061UKWH00001BB/44

9 798218 214685